Psalms
for Sadness, Sickness and Celebration

Text by Richard Gordon
Photographs by Pearl Hutchinson

Printed & Published by
Impact Publishers
Coleraine & Ballycastle

Copyright Photographs Pearl Hutchinson 2003
Copyright Prayers Dr. Richard Gordon 2003

Second Edition 2004

ISBN. 0 948154 34 9

In this book I have selected twenty short psalms which have sustained and intrigued, calmed and mystified, entertained, inspired and even infuriated millions of believers for thousands of years. Some are very well known and others seldom heard or read in public.

Each psalm is accompanied by a photograph in order to suggest something of what it says to us. In addition there is a prayer arising from the content of the psalm.

There are psalms for every human mood, so no matter what we are feeling the psalmist has been there before us. Joy and sadness, despair and hope, confusion and anger – these and many other emotions are all addressed.

These twenty psalms with their accompanying illustrations are like beautiful pearls on a string. As you handle each one, I hope that its wonder will rub off on you.

Dick Gordon

Acknowledgments

We are grateful for the help and encouragement we have received from many people in the production of this book.

Our thanks go to Tenia Woods. Tenia was very much part of this project from the beginning, co-ordinating our efforts and doing her best to keep us in line.

A special word of thanks goes to Professor Harold Nicholl who read the script and wrote the Foreword. He also made some valuable suggestions.

Our families were hugely supportive offering advice and encouragement when we needed it most and they also helped us to market the book!

Thanks go to Impact Printing for their professional help in getting the book printed and for giving us the confidence to keep going.

The entire first edition has been sold and all the profit is being devoted to the welfare of people in the Churches in Zomba. This is being effected through ZAP, the Zomba Action Project, a charity which arose from the link which exists between Coleraine Borough Council in Northern Ireland and the Zomba Municipal Authority in Southern Malawi.

Any profit achieved by this Second Edition will also be used for missionary purposes in Malawi.

I first heard the psalms sung in a very traditional way almost fifty years ago in a little church in Co. Donegal. My grandfather was the precentor. He especially liked to sing the psalms when he was out in the fields or when he sat by the fire in the evening. The God that he worshipped was the same God that the psalmist had worshipped.

For me the presence of that same God of the psalms can still be seen all around us. The photographs in this book were taken mostly around my home. Some will be familiar and others are favourite places of mine. I hope that as you read this book the beauty of God's world will help you reflect on the words of the psalmist.

O taste and see that the Lord is good.
Psalm 34 v.8

Pearl Hutchinson

Foreword

The many people who have found in the Book of Psalms a rich source of inspiration, challenge and consolation will warmly welcome this little volume. It contains 20 psalms chosen by Dr Richard Gordon with a short meditation accompanying each one. Dr Gordon is uniquely qualified for this task by his long experience in Old Testament scholarship and by his very obvious human qualities of understanding, insight and deep compassion for human frailty.

Each psalm is illustrated by a photograph from Mrs Pearl Hutchinson which amplifies the verbal message with what Bishop Berkeley called "the Divine visual language" of the world around us. Pearl has been very successful in matching the scenes with the thoughts of the Psalmist and readers will, I am sure, agree that here again the words have been greatly reinforced by the pictures.

We are much in their debt and I warmly commend the book to a wide circle of readers.

Professor Harold Nicholl

All the photographs in this book were taken in Counties Londonderry and Donegal.

The twenty psalms quoted are all taken from The Holy Bible, New International Version.

Doing it God's way

Psalm 1

Blessed is the man
who does not walk in the counsel of the wicked
or stand in the way of sinners
or sit in the seat of mockers.
But his delight is in the law of the Lord
and on his law he meditates day and night.
He is like a tree planted by streams of water,
which yields its fruit in season
and whose leaf does not wither.
Whatever he does prospers.

Not so the wicked!
They are like chaff
that the wind blows away.
Therefore the wicked will not stand in the judgment,
nor sinners in the assembly of the righteous.

For the Lord watches over the way of the righteous,
but the way of the wicked will perish.

Prayer
Thank you Lord for the Ten
Commandments
We know that they are not harsh
impositions but rather your invitation
to live life your way.
It is wonderful God to be in right
relationships with others and even
more so to be in a right relationship
with You.
Grant us the courage and the strength
to resist temptation and to follow You,
for Jesus' sake.
Amen.

Agivey River at Cullycapple Bridge, Aghadowey.

He is like a tree planted by streams of water.

Talking things over with the Lord.

Psalm 4

Answer me when I call to you,
O my righteous God.
Give me relief from my distress;
be merciful to me and hear my prayer.

How long, O men, will you turn my glory into shame?
How long will you love delusions and seek false gods?

Know that the Lord has set apart the godly for himself;
the Lord will hear when I call to him.

In your anger do not sin;
when you are on your beds,
search your hearts and be silent.

Offer right sacrifices
and trust in the Lord

Many are asking, "Who can show us any good?"
Let the light of your face shine upon us, O Lord .
You have filled my heart with greater joy
than when their grain and new wine abound.
I will lie down and sleep in peace,
for you alone, O Lord ,
make me dwell in safety.

Prayer
Lord in your Word You and I can talk
things over.
This is great!
I know I'm cross too often and quite
often unreasonable!
But when I talk things over with You,
God, life makes more sense.
When I talk to You, You are close again
and I can go peacefully to sleep.
Lord You put me together.
Amen

Rathmullan Beach.

The Lord will hear when I call to him.

I'm sick Lord

Psalm 6

*O Lord, do not rebuke me in your anger
or discipline me in your wrath.
Be merciful to me, Lord, for I am faint;
O Lord, heal me, for my bones are in agony.
My soul is in anguish.
How long, O Lord, how long?*

*Turn, O Lord, and deliver me;
save me because of your unfailing love.
No one remembers you when he is dead.
Who praises you from his grave ?*

*I am worn out from groaning;
all night long I flood my bed with weeping
and drench my couch with tears.
My eyes grow weak with sorrow;
they fail because of all my foes.*

*Away from me, all you who do evil,
for the Lord has heard my weeping.
The Lord has heard my cry for mercy;
the Lord accepts my prayer.
All my enemies will be ashamed and dismayed;
they will turn back in sudden disgrace.*

Prayer
Father in heaven, hear my prayers.
I'm sick, I'm sad, I'm fed up!
But I know you help when I admit my
mistakes, and confess my sins.
You pick me up when I fall down.
You give me another chance when I say,
'Sorry, Lord'.
You hear me out when the world will
not listen.
When I am walking with you Lord, I'm
walking tall!
In Jesus Name,
Amen.

The lights of Buncrana from Rathmullan.

O Lord heal me for my bones are in agony.

Your world is amazing Lord

Psalm 8

O Lord, our Lord,
how majestic is your name in all the earth!

You have set your glory
above the heavens.
From the lips of children and infants
you have ordained praise
because of your enemies,
to silence the foe and the avenger.

When I consider your heavens,
the work of your fingers,
the moon and the stars,
which you have set in place,
what is man that you are mindful of him,
the son of man that you care for him?
You made him a little lower than the heavenly beings
and crowned him with glory and honour.

You made him ruler over the works of your hands;
you put everything under his feet:
all flocks and herds,
and the beasts of the field,
the birds of the air,
and the fish of the sea,
all that swim the paths of the seas.
O Lord, our Lord,
how majestic is your name in all the earth!

Prayer
We are your handiwork, Lord Jesus.
The birds, the bees, the lions and the trees,
The wonder of the macro and the mega and the fascination of the micro and the miniscule.
You made them all!
Lord help us to be good stewards of your world, conserving for You and for succeeding generations.
Thank You for loving our world and delighting in the praise of children.
Amen

Anemones in Movanagher Wood, Kilrea.

What is man that you are mindful of him?

Sometimes it's very dark

Psalm 13

How long, O Lord? Will you forget me forever?
How long will you hide your face from me?
How long must I wrestle with my thoughts
and every day have sorrow in my heart?
How long will my enemy triumph over me?

Look on me and answer, O Lord my God.
Give light to my eyes, or I will sleep in death;
my enemy will say, "I have overcome him,"
and my foes will rejoice when I fall.

But I trust in your unfailing love;
my heart rejoices in your salvation.
I will sing to the Lord,
for he has been good to me.

Prayer
Sorry, Lord! I'm so impatient!
I need your help and your presence
and I need them now!
I need your answer to my prayer.
Lord, there is so much that I need.
You are the unfailing one who is so
good to all who call upon your Name.
You forgive, restore and enable all who
ask in Jesus' name.
 Amen

Sunset over the River Bann at Portna, Kilrea.

How long must I wrestle with my thoughts?

Are you really there Lord?

Psalm 14

The fool says in his heart,
"There is no God."
They are corrupt, their deeds are vile;
there is no one who does good.

The Lord looks down from heaven
on the sons of men
to see if there are any who understand,
any who seek God.
All have turned aside,
they have together become corrupt;
there is no one who does good,
not even one.

Will evildoers never learn-
those who devour my people as men eat bread
and who do not call on the Lord ?
There they are, overwhelmed with dread,
for God is present in the company of the righteous.
You evildoers frustrate the plans of the poor,
but the Lord is their refuge.

Oh, that salvation for Israel would come out of Zion!
When the Lord restores the fortunes of his people,
let Jacob rejoice and Israel be glad!

Prayer
We rejoice in You Lord!
You are in charge and Christ will be
returning in glory!
Thank you Lord Jesus for light at the
end of the tunnel.
Amen.

Bridge over the River Bann at Kilrea.

The Lord looks down from heaven

I'm glad that you are near Lord

Psalm 16

Keep me safe, O God,
for in you I take refuge.

I said to the Lord , "You are my Lord;
apart from you I have no good thing."
As for the saints who are in the land,
they are the glorious ones in whom is all my delight.
The sorrows of those will increase
who run after other gods.
I will not pour out their libations of blood
or take up their names on my lips.

Lord, you have assigned me my portion and my cup;
you have made my lot secure.
The boundary lines have fallen for me in pleasant places;
surely I have a delightful inheritance.

I will praise the Lord, who counsels me;
even at night my heart instructs me.
I have set the Lord always before me.
Because he is at my right hand,
I shall not be shaken.

Therefore my heart is glad and my tongue rejoices;
my body also will rest secure,
because you will not abandon me to the grave,
nor will you let your Holy One see decay.
You have made known to me the path of life;
you will fill me with joy in your presence,
with eternal pleasures at your right hand.

Prayer
Thank You Lord, for being so strong
Thank You Lord for being present with
us always.
Thank You Lord for being You for me,
and for us.
Amen.

Daffodil garden at the University of Ulster, Coleraine.

The boundary lines have fallen for me in pleasant places

Lord, you are my shepherd.

Psalm 23

The Lord is my shepherd, I shall not be in want.
He makes me lie down in green pastures,
he leads me beside quiet waters,
he restores my soul.
He guides me in paths of righteousness
for his name's sake.
Even though I walk
through the valley of the shadow of death,
I will fear no evil,
for you are with me;
your rod and your staff,
they comfort me.

You prepare a table before me
in the presence of my enemies.
You anoint my head with oil;
my cup overflows.
Surely goodness and love will follow me
all the days of my life,
and I will dwell in the house of the Lord
for ever.

Prayer
Our Father we give You praise and
thanks!
We thank You for the provision for our
needs, and for protection, for we are so
vulnerable.
Even when we are frightened and seem
to be alone, we can rejoice in the
assurance of your Presence and the
power of your Word.
You are both our shepherd and our
host, you watch over us at the glad
times, the sad times and the lonely
times.
You are nearer than our closest friend
and your sure promises to believers
remind us that in the Father's House
there are many rooms.
Amen

Agivey River at Hunter's Mill, Aghadowey.

Beside quiet waters

Our world is your world

Psalm 24

The earth is the Lord's, and everything in it,
the world, and all who live in it;
for he founded it upon the seas
and established it upon the waters.

Who may ascend the hill of the Lord ?
Who may stand in his holy place?
He who has clean hands and a pure heart,
who does not lift up his soul to an idol
or swear by what is false.
He will receive blessing from the Lord
and vindication from God his Saviour.
Such is the generation of those who seek him,
who seek your face, O God of Jacob.

Lift up your heads, O you gates;
be lifted up, you ancient doors,
that the King of glory may come in.
Who is this King of glory?
The Lord strong and mighty,
the Lord mighty in battle.
Lift up your heads, O you gates;
lift them up, you ancient doors,
that the King of glory may come in.
Who is he, this King of glory?
The Lord Almighty-
he is the King of glory.

Prayer
Lord, we celebrate creation and
salvation in our praises.
Let us lift up hearts and heads and
invite the King to enter in.
Lord we are not very strong, not very
good, not very brave, but we are your
people.
We are the flock of your hand, indeed
the 'apples of your eye' and we are
your guests, by the grace and goodness
of Jesus.
Amen.

Mulroy Bay.

Lift up your heads, O you gates

You give me courage.

Psalm 46

God is our refuge and strength,
an ever-present help in trouble.
Therefore we will not fear, though the earth give way
and the mountains fall into the heart of the sea,
though its waters roar and foam
and the mountains quake with their surging.

There is a river whose streams make glad the city of God,
the holy place where the Most High dwells.
God is within her, she will not fall;
God will help her at break of day.
Nations are in uproar, kingdoms fall;
he lifts his voice, the earth melts.

The Lord Almighty is with us;
the God of Jacob is our fortress.

Come and see the works of the Lord,
the desolations he has brought on the earth.
He makes wars cease to the ends of the earth;
he breaks the bow and shatters the spear,
he burns the shields with fire.
"Be still, and know that I am God;
I will be exalted among the nations,
I will be exalted in the earth."

The Lord Almighty is with us;
the God of Jacob is our fortress.

Prayer
Lord in an unholy world plagued by
disasters, violence and wars, we
rejoice to claim that our God is a safe
stronghold.
We praise your name O Lord.
We rely upon your power.
We enjoy your forgiveness.
We long for your peace.
Keep us mindful of our duty and
faithful in our devotions.
For we praise the name of Jesus.
Amen

Beech tree at Greenvale, Drumagarner, Kilrea.

*God is our refuge
and strength*

It's good to be at home with the Lord.

Psalm 84

How lovely is your dwelling - place,
O Lord Almighty!
My soul yearns, even faints,
for the courts of the Lord ;
my heart and my flesh cry out
for the living God.

Even the sparrow has found a home,
and the swallow a nest for herself,
where she may have her young-
a place near your altar,
O Lord Almighty, my King and my God.
Blessed are those who dwell in your house;
they are ever praising you.

Blessed are those whose strength is in you,
who have set their hearts on pilgrimage.
As they pass through the Valley of Baca,
they make it a place of springs;
the autumn rains also cover it with pools.
They go from strength to strength,
till each appears before God in Zion.

Hear my prayer, O Lord God Almighty;
listen to me, O God of Jacob.

Look upon our shield, O God;
look with favour on your anointed one.

Better is one day in your courts
than a thousand elsewhere;
I would rather be a doorkeeper in the house of my God
than dwell in the tents of the wicked.
For the Lord God is a sun and shield;
the Lord bestows favour and honour;
no good thing does he withhold
from those whose walk is blameless.

O Lord Almighty,
blessed is the man who trusts in you.

Prayer.
Lord grant that we may travel safely
on every part of life's journey. May
your house be our refuge at every stage
and may we always live within the
security of your presence.
For it is lovely to live with the Lord, to
know his blessing, and anticipate his
eternity in Christ.
Lord be our certainty in an uncertain
world.
Amen.

21

First Derry Presbyterian Church.

I would rather be a door keeper in the house of my God

God – you are for ever!

Psalm 93

The Lord reigns, he is robed in majesty;
the Lord is robed in majesty
and is armed with strength.
The world is firmly established;
it cannot be moved.
Your throne was established long ago;
you are from all eternity.

The seas have lifted up, O Lord ,
the seas have lifted up their voice;
the seas have lifted up their pounding waves.
Mightier than the thunder of the great waters,
mightier than the breakers of the sea-
the Lord on high is mighty.

Your statutes stand firm;
holiness adorns your house
for endless days, O Lord .

Prayer
Lord the mystery of your majesty is all
around and beyond.
Your reign stretches back to the very
beginning.
You as Holy Spirit are powerfully
present even now.
The future of eternity is with you.
Lord you are stronger than the
mightiest wave and your way is sure.
And your Son Jesus Christ revealed to
us that he is the Way, the Truth and the
Life.
Amen.

From the Promenade, Portstewart.

The Lord reigns, he is robed in majesty

Thank you God.

Psalm 100

Shout for joy to the Lord , all the earth.
Worship the Lord with gladness;
come before him with joyful songs.
Know that the Lord is God.
It is he who made us, and we are his ;
we are his people, the sheep of his pasture.

Enter his gates with thanksgiving
and his courts with praise;
give thanks to him and praise his name.
For the Lord is good and his love endures forever;
his faithfulness continues through all generations.

Prayer
Thanks be to You O God, for your
wonderful creation, preservation and
salvation.
You made us.
You sustain us.
You save us.
You made the world, all your creation
and everyone in all nations.
Your salvation offer extends to all
mankind.
Jesus is our guarantee.
Hallelujah.
Amen.

The Bishop's Gate, Downhill.

Enter his gates with thanksgiving, and his courts with praise

This is His song

Psalm 101

I will sing of your love and justice;
to you, O Lord, I will sing praise.
I will be careful to lead a blameless life-
when will you come to me?

I will walk in my house
with blameless heart.
I will set before my eyes
no vile thing.

The deeds of faithless men I hate;
they will not cling to me.
Men of perverse heart shall be far from me;
I will have nothing to do with evil.

Whoever slanders his neighbour in secret,
him will I put to silence;
whoever has haughty eyes and a proud heart,
him will I not endure.

My eyes will be on the faithful in the land,
that they may dwell with me;
he whose walk is blameless
will minister to me.

No one who practices deceit
will dwell in my house;
no one who speaks falsely
will stand in my presence.

Every morning I will put to silence
all the wicked in the land;
I will cut off every evildoer
from the city of the Lord.

Prayer
Lord God grant us a beautiful humility
and a passion for integrity, peace and
justice.
In you Lord God and in your Son Jesus
Christ we see the way to live life
gloriously to your honour and praise.
It is good for us to sit with Jesus and
allow ourselves to hear his voice.
This psalm becomes Messiah's looking
forward to his reign in his redeemed
world.
Jesus my God and my King.
Amen

The grounds of Fort Royal Hotel, Rathmullan.

He whose walk is blameless will minister to me

Who is the Lord?

Psalm 110

The Lord says to my Lord:
"Sit at my right hand
until I make your enemies
a footstool for your feet."

The Lord will extend your mighty sceptre from Zion;
you will rule in the midst of your enemies.
Your troops will be willing
on your day of battle.
Arrayed in holy majesty,
from the womb of the dawn
you will receive the dew of your youth.

The Lord has sworn
and will not change his mind:
"You are a priest forever,
in the order of Melchizedek."

The Lord is at your right hand;
he will crush kings on the day of his wrath.
He will judge nations, heaping up the dead
and crushing the rulers of the whole earth.
He will drink from a brook beside the way;
therefore he will lift up his head.

Prayer
Jesus, We rejoice that you declared
God's prophetic Word, and that you
were both priest and willing sacrifice
upon the Cross and that you rule as
King on High.
You are Prophet, Priest and King, You
are Saviour, and we are able to call
you Friend.
Hallelujah!
Amen.

Looking towards Cottage Grove, Kilrea.

You will rule in the midst of your enemies

Are you listening, Lord?

Psalm 130

Out of the depths I cry to you, O Lord ;
O Lord, hear my voice.
Let your ears be attentive
to my cry for mercy.

If you, O Lord, kept a record of sins,
O Lord, who could stand?
But with you there is forgiveness;
therefore you are feared.

I wait for the Lord , my soul waits,
and in his word I put my hope.
My soul waits for the Lord
more than watchmen wait for the morning,
more than watchmen wait for the morning.

O Israel, put your hope in the Lord ,
for with the Lord is unfailing love
and with him is full redemption.
He himself will redeem Israel
from all their sins.

Prayer
Thank you God for listening to all my
prayers.
Thank you Lord for forgiving my sins.
Thank you Lord for being the Hope of
the world and my Hope.
Grant to us the patience required to
wait upon the Lord, and to renew our
strength.
In Jesus Name,
Amen.

From my home in Kilrea.

Out of the depths I cry to you, O Lord

Families are precious.

Psalm 133

How good and pleasant it is
when brothers live together in unity!
It is like precious oil poured on the head,
running down on the beard,
running down on Aaron's beard,
down upon the collar of his robes.
It is as if the dew of Hermon
were falling on Mount Zion.
For there the Lord bestows his blessing,
even life for evermore.

Prayer
To live in unity is a wonderful blessing.
Blessed are the peacemakers for they
shall see God.
Lord make me a reconciler.
For Jesus' sake, Amen

Rathmullan.

How good and pleasant it is when brothers dwell in unity

Count your blessings!

Psalm 134

Praise the Lord, all you servants of the Lord
who minister by night in the house of the Lord.
Lift up your hands in the sanctuary
and praise the Lord.

May the Lord, the Maker of heaven and earth,
bless you from Zion.

Prayer
We praise you Lord and you bless us!
Thanks be to the God and Father of our
Lord Jesus Christ who has won for us
such a wonderful salvation!
Lord we confess our inadequacy but
rejoice in our high calling to be your
servants.
Lord make us good servants who
rejoice in their calling.
Amen

St.Patrick's Parish Church, Coleraine.

May the Lord, the Maker of heaven and earth, bless you from Zion.

Can I really praise you Lord in difficult places?

Psalm 137
By the rivers of Babylon we sat and wept
when we remembered Zion.
There on the poplars
we hung our harps,
for there our captors asked us for songs,
our tormentors demanded songs of joy;
they said, "Sing us one of the songs of Zion!"

How can we sing the songs of the Lord
while in a foreign land?
If I forget you, O Jerusalem,
may my right hand forget its skill .
May my tongue cling to the roof of my mouth
if I do not remember you,
if I do not consider Jerusalem
my highest joy.

Remember, O Lord , what the Edomites did
on the day Jerusalem fell.
"Tear it down," they cried,
"tear it down to its foundations!"

O Daughter of Babylon, doomed to destruction,
happy is he who repays you
for what you have done to us-
he who seizes your infants
and dashes them against the rocks.

Prayer
When the Children of Israel were in
captivity in Babylon they found it hard
to worship.
Lord help us to remember you when we
are in difficult situations.
Prayer and praise do not always come
easily, yet as your children, we were
made for prayer and praise.
Grant Loving Lord that the praise of
our lips and the service of our lives
may be beautiful in your sight.
For Jesus' sake -
Amen

Windmill, Drumagarner, Kilrea.

Can I really praise you Lord in difficult places?

I'm a Christian, I can hear Jesus through the Old Testament

Psalm 146

Praise the Lord .
Praise the Lord, O my soul.
I will praise the Lord all my life;
I will sing praise to my God as long as I live.

Do not put your trust in princes,
in mortal men, who cannot save.
When their spirit departs, they return to the ground;
on that very day their plans come to nothing.

Blessed is he whose help is the God of Jacob,
whose hope is in the Lord his God,
the Maker of heaven and earth,
the sea, and everything in them-
the Lord, who remains faithful forever.
He upholds the cause of the oppressed
and gives food to the hungry.
The Lord sets prisoners free,
the Lord gives sight to the blind,
the Lord lifts up those who are bowed down,
the Lord loves the righteous.
The Lord watches over the alien
and sustains the fatherless and the widow,
but he frustrates the ways of the wicked.

The Lord reigns forever,
your God, O Zion, for all generations.

Praise the Lord.

Prayer
Thank you God that the promised
Saviour came to earth as Jesus.
May we share his concerns and live
our lives in the constant praise He gave
to the Father.
Speak to us Lord that we may hear,
and give us the grace to follow Jesus.
Amen.

Mussenden Temple, Downhill.

The Lord gives sight to the blind